He Was In The World

John L. Bell

Meditations for public worship

First published 1995

ISBN 0 947988 70 X

Cover and illustrations by Graham Maule

Text and illustrations
© 1995, Wild Goose Resource Group, Iona Community

Wild Goose Publications
Unit 15, Six Harmony Row, Glasgow G51 3BA

Wild Goose Publications is the publishing division
of the Iona Community.

Scottish Charity No. SCO03794. Limited Company Reg. No. SCO96243.

A catalogue record for this book is available from the British Library.

Extracts from the Psalms are abridged from the Good News Bible
published by the Bible Societies/HarperCollins Publishers Ltd UK
© American Bible Society 1966, 1971, 1976, 1992,
Used with permission.

We gratefully acknowledge the contribution of

THE DRUMMOND TRUST
3 PITT TERRACE, STIRLING

towards the publication costs of this book.

Printed in Great Britain by The Cromwell Press, Melksham, Wiltshire

*C*ontents

I n t r o d u c t i o n

These meditations have been many years in the making. They were developed as circumstances required for a variety of conferences, church services and other events throughout Britain.

They are essentially public material, written to be read where people are gathered, rather than for private devotional use. They require one or more people to read, who often must forgo any personal benefit, in order that a group or congregation can enter into the story.

They are not poems, nor are they the kind of spiritual readings that someone in search of a 'filler' for opening devotions or an epilogue can use at a moment's notice. If that is the kind of thing you are after, you have the wrong book.

Each meditation will need preparation and rehearsal, even if that simply means reading it over aloud before using it. To stumble through a reading in worship (be it Scripture or otherwise) is not fair on those who depend on the leader's words. God will honour our preparation, even if most people will not be aware of it.

Equally, each meditation should be used in an appropriate context. By this, three things are implied:

T h e m a t i c

The meditations cover a range of personal, pastoral and biblical themes. While it might be 'nice' to read 'The Starfish' at any time, if there is no focus on the ministry of healing during the time of worship, then there is no context in which to use it. There should be an integrity between the theme of the meditation and other components of worship.

L i t u r g i c a l

Some of the meditations immediately suggest where they could be used in an act of worship. 'Fourspeak' for example, might take the place of a sermon. 'The Stranger' might be best placed just before the prayer of consecration at Holy Communion.

Others, such as 'On the Bus' might be the basis for a short epilogue with a song before and a prayer and song to follow.

To use them imaginatively, we have to think beyond merely inserting them into our order of worship as extras, but rather finding what they can replace or complement, or what might complement them.

Architectural

The place from which a meditation is read is important. The pulpit or lectern at the front is not necessarily where all reading should take place.

For a sermon, the preacher has to be seen and make eye contact with the congregation. But meditation is a different experience. And to let it be an experience, attention has to be paid to how people sit and where they sit; where the various voices should speak from and what, if any, should be a focal point.

The mention of focal point leads to two particular aspects of the meditations.

The first is that many of them encourage the use of symbols, candles, a centrally positioned cross etc. Some worshippers (especially Protestants) may needlessly feel uneasy about this. It will help to reassure them that God biblically communicates with people through the sight or use of symbols – of which fire, rainbows, stones and seeds are the more obvious. It is our perennial experience that for many people taking part in an activity that involves signs and symbols has a great spiritual value that is quite different from listening to prayers and preaching. And it is especially welcomed by people whose needs are poorly served by 'wordbound' forms of worship.

Secondly, several of the meditations involve the use of meditative verse songs (or chants) and responses. These are employed because they break up the narrative and because the simplicity of the words and tunes allows people to use them either for reflection or for movement in a way that is impossible with a five-verse hymn. Suitable songs are listed in the preface to the meditation. Three kinds have been chosen – songs from the Taizé Community, from the World Church and from the Iona Community. Information about the availability of the music is given in an appendix.

One final word of encouragement and caution: please do not use these meditations either in sequence or in close proximity to each other. One per act of worship is enough, but not every act of worship, epilogue or whatever needs to have one. If it takes five years to use every item in the book, that will be approximately the time it took to devise them.

It is our deep hope that the material in this collection will bring its users into a fond and lively relationship with the God who was in the world and who still meets us in it.

John L. Bell
July 1994

*P*astoral

THE STARFISH [1]

This is one of three meditations that can be used at services of healing or to encourage people to think about wholeness. Its theme is the need for the strong to care for the weak, and for the well integrated to care for the forgotten. It should be read slowly by one person. There is a break before the end (†). This indicates how the meditation was originally used: a reader read the words up to the break; the leader of worship gave a reflection on Christ's healing ministry; and then the meditation was read again, this time right to the end. It is sufficient, however, for the piece to be read as a whole.

In the morning early,
I saw the folk from the village
combing the sand for starfish
which the waves had washed up
and left vulnerable.

These, the villagers would collect, kill,
and sell for profit.
That was their way.

One morning I rose earlier,
and walked on the sand by the water's edge.

There, in the distance, I saw a solitary figure
who was also looking for starfish.

Whenever he found one alive or even just alive,
he would lift it, kiss it,
and lay it back in the blue water,
there to be revived and to swim again.
That was his way.

Now I get up every morning,
earlier than the villagers,
early as the man.
I, the strong, no longer stretch to survive:
I kneel down to restore the weak. †

And I have found,
though some might mock me,
that even far from the seaside,
there are starfish on every street.

1 'The Starfish' is based on a story by Loren Eiseley from *The Promise of Paradox* (Servant Leadership Press, Washinton DC, 1993) by Parker J. Palmer. Reproduced by permission.

THE CLOWN

*This meditation for a service of healing or reconciliation deals with
the person of Christ, the original fool for God, who delights those
who are patronizingly pitied and meets us at the point of our own
need.*

It was eight in the evening
when we came to the fairground,
the clown and I.

We had hardly arrived,
when there was a hysterical scream.
Down the helter skelter
came a 10 year old girl in callipers
her face aglow with delight.

On our right was a caravan.
I looked in
to see a fortune teller
gazing at the palm of a woman with Aids.
Both were smiling.

Round and round spun the rib tickler
and when eventually it stopped,
out staggered two manic depressives,
splitting their sides with laughter.

On a chair with a rifle cocked in his toes,
an armless ex-soldier was hitting the jackpot
and winning major prizes.

So I turned on the clown and said,
'This is absurd!'
I turned and said,
'This is perverse!'
I turned and said,
'This is obscene!'

'Who else gives them the time of their lives?'
asked the clown.

'Who else gives the best to the least?'

And he nodded to a roundabout
where my neighbour, still dressed for the office,
bobbed up and down on a unicorn's back.

'What's he doing here?' I asked.
'There's nothing wrong with him!' I said.

'There are some things you don't know,' came the reply.
And just at that, the roundabout stopped.

All seats were emptied,
and all were taken
apart from one.

As we drew near,
I saw my name on the saddle.
'But how did you know?' I asked.

And the clown smiled softly.

THE TEACHERS

This meditation deals with the necessary interaction between those who seem to be deprived or disabled and those who think that they are alright.

The words should be read by one voice. It may be helpful to have appropriate music played under the reading. Another option is a short musical interlude where a pause in the narrative is indicated.

I met him on the train,
and before long I felt I knew him,
I felt I could trust him.

He was in education: 'Learning for Life' he called it.

I said I was interested in education too,
so he invited me to come with him
to where he taught and learned.

It was off the main road, near the fire station.
It didn't look like a school ...
You walked in the door of a second-hand shop
and, going through the back,
you came to a big room with a lot of people in it.
We stood and looked around.

    (Pause)

In the corner was an old man with a white stick.
Beside him sat a girl reading him the newspaper.

'Nice to see young folk helping the blind,' I said.
'Oh,' he replied, 'he's actually teaching her how to see.'

Across the floor, in the direction of the toilets,
came a wheelchair.
A paraplegic boy of 18 sat in it
and a boy the same age pushed it.

'It's great when friends help each other,' I said.
'Yes,' he replied, 'the boy in the chair
is teaching the other how to walk.'

An old woman lay in a bed at the bottom of the room.
She was covered with open sores.
A woman, much her junior, was dressing her wounds.

'Is she a nurse?' I asked.
'Yes,' he replied, 'the old woman is a nurse.
She's teaching the other how to care.'

Seated round a table were a group of young couples.
A doctor in a white coat was talking to them about childbirth.
He spoke slowly and used sign language with his hands.

'I think it's only fair
that deaf people should know about these things,' I said.
'But they do know about these things,' my friend replied.
'They are teaching the doctor how to listen.'

And then I saw a woman on a respirator, breathing slowly.
These were her last breaths.
And around her were her friends, smoothing her brow,
holding her hands.

'It's not good to die alone,' I said.
'That's right,' he replied,
'but she is not dying alone.
She is teaching the others how to live.'

Confused and not knowing what to say,
I suggested we sat down.

    (Pause)

After a while, I felt I could speak.
'Seeing all this,' I said, 'I want to pray.
I want to thank God that I have all my faculties.
I now realize how much I can do to help.'

Before I could say more,
he looked me straight in the face and said,
'I don't want to upset your devotional life,
but I hope you will also pray
to know your own need.

And I hope you will never be afraid
to be touched by the needy.'

I NEVER WANTED TO BE BORN

Written originally for the funeral service of a group of teenagers who had been killed in a car crash, this meditation is suitable for similar acts of worship, especially where death has been sudden and tragic.

It should be read slowly.

I never wanted to be born.

The older I grew,
the fonder I became
of my mother's womb
and its warmth
and its safety.

I feared the unknown:
        the next world,
about which I knew nothing
but imagined the worst.

Yet, as I grew older,
I sensed in my soul
that the womb was not my home forever.

Though I did not know when,
I felt sure that one day
I would disappear through a door
which had yet to be opened,
and confront the unknown
of which I was afraid.

And then,
it happened.

In blood, tears and pain,
it happened.

I was cut off from the familiar;
I left my life behind

and discovered not darkness but light,
        not hostility but love,
        not eternal separation
but hands that wanted to hold me.

      (Pause)

I never wanted to be born.

I don't want to die.

The older I grow,
the fonder I become
of this world
and its warmth
and its safety.

I fear the unknown:
      the next world,
about which I know nothing
but imagine the worst.

Yet as I grow older,
I sense in my soul
that this world is not my home forever.

Though I do not know when,
I feel that one day
I will disappear through a door
which has yet to be opened.

Perhaps having come so safely through the first door,
I should not fear so hopelessly the second.

F O U R S P E A K

The prospect of leading a Remembrance Sunday service does not always invoke enthusiasm. In any congregation there may be gathered women who were widowed because of the war; men who were in the armed forces during the war; and people, middle-aged and younger, for whom 1939–45 is not a memory and whose attitudes to nuclear deterrence may be advertised on their lapel badges.

It was such a prospect which gave rise to this meditation. Rather than have a sermon which would reflect where the preacher felt people should be, these words reflected where people came from, and were put together drawing on the experience of very different individuals.

They were read between the Old Testament lesson and the gospel, allowing the words of the gospel to respond to the diversity of experience and understanding in the people.

Outside a worship context, the material may be of use in discussion groups on peace issues, where past experience has to be reckoned with in understanding present attitudes.

Whether used inside or outside of a worship context, the readers should, as far as possible, be the same sex as their characters and near the same age. They should be scattered among the congregation. Local allusions, names of regiments and people etc, may be changed to suit. The ages of the characters will have to be brought up to date according to the year you use the script.

JOHN: I'm John and I'm 85.

RITA: I'm Rita and I'm 65.

HENRY: I'm Henry and I'm 45.

TRACY: I'm Tracy and I'm 19.

JOHN: When I was 5, Britain entered the First World War.

RITA: When I was 10, Britain entered the Second World War.

HENRY: I'm one of what was called the post-war bulge.

TRACY: I'm Tracy and I'm 19.

(Pause)

JOHN: I was the youngest of a family of ten.
Eight of us were boys.
Three – Hugh, Charlie and Andrew –
were miners like my father.
They never got called up.
But Dave and Rab did.

RITA: My father was over 50 in 1939.
He was too old for the regular army,
so they made him a sergeant-major
in the Home Guard.
He used to send my mother postcards
from weekend camps at Carnoustie.
But my brothers – Alastair and Jackie –
they got called up
and my father was really proud,
especially when Alastair got his wings in the RAF.

HENRY: My father got demobbed in 1948.
He never saw any action.
He was in the Scots Guards
and they got sent into Poland and Italy
to do the clearing up after Hitler and Mussolini fell.

TRACY: My big brother has two cases full of war comics.

(Pause)

JOHN: Dave was killed in the Dardanelles.
Rab froze to death in Siberia.

RITA: Alastair was shot down over Dresden.
Jackie spent three years
in a Japanese prisoner-of-war camp.
He's been in a mental hospital ever since.

JOHN: My father blamed Churchill.

RITA: My father blamed himself.

HENRY: My father never saw any action.

TRACY: My father used to be in CND.
He sometimes talks about the sixties ...
Bob Dylan and Joan Baez
and all the protest songs about the war in Vietnam.

My father once nearly got arrested for demonstrating
outside the American Embassy in London.
My mother told me that.

RITA: My mother told me
that the Japs were worse than the Germans.
But she never told me
what Alastair was doing at Dresden.
She never told me my brother bombed civilians.

HENRY: My mother told me
that my father got married in his demob suit,
and everybody in the street
gave my gran their sugar rations for the week
so that she could ice the wedding cake
and have nice things at the reception.

TRACY: My mother used to be in CND too.
She got Bruce Kent's photograph
when he was still a priest.

(Pause)

JOHN: I still have our Dave's Bible.
They sent it back with his medals
and a note from his CO
saying he should have won the VC.

His name's on the memorial at the side of the church.
So is Rab's.

RITA: I was at church the morning they declared war.
Everybody knew it was going to happen.

It was halfway through the third hymn.
Jimmy McMaster had been listening

to the wireless in the vestry.
He came into the church
and walked up the pulpit stairs
and whispered the news to the minister.

Everybody stopped singing.
There was just the organ playing.

HENRY: My father refused to get married in a church.
Just before he got demobbed he went to Marburg
where the Protestants put swastikas
over the communion tables.

He said the Catholics were just as bad.
The Vatican never stood up to Mussolini.

TRACY: I once heard Bruce Kent speak.
He kept talking about Jesus
and bits from the Old Testament.
I thought he'd have given that up when he got married.

(Pause)

JOHN: 'The war to end all wars' ...
but then there was the Second World War –

RITA: and then there was Suez –

HENRY: and then there was Vietnam –

TRACY: and then there was the Falklands –

JOHN: and the Russian invasion of Czechoslovakia –

RITA: and the American invasion of Grenada –

HENRY: and the Israeli invasion of the West Bank –

TRACY: and the Iraqi invasion of Kuwait –

JOHN: and Wenceslas Square –

RITA: and Tiananmen Square –

HENRY: and Nicaragua and South Africa –

TRACY: and Bosnia and Somalia.

JOHN: 'The war to end all wars' ...
I'll never forget it.

RITA: I'll never forgive it.

HENRY: I'll never understand it.

TRACY: I'll be 20 next month.

JOHN: We were all young once.

RITA: They don't know how lucky they are.

HENRY: I'll never understand it.

TRACY: My name is Tracy and I'm 19.

(The above may be appropriately followed by reading Matt. 24.4-14.)

Personal

THE RABBIT HUTCH

If possible, don't mention in advance the name of this meditation, but do indicate that it is one in which there will be a time for quiet personal prayer followed by a sung response.

It requires people to close their eyes and use their imaginations. So ensure that people feel comfortable before beginning to read it. Only one voice is required for the narrative. A second person may be designated to begin the song.

If there is to be no singing, a respectful silence at the appropriate place may be sufficient.

SUITABLE SONGS (SEE PAGE 104)
WATCH AND PRAY (WGRG, IONA COMMUNITY)
O LORD, HEAR MY PRAYER (TAIZÉ)

Imagine yourself walking down the main street
of a country town, at about ten o'clock in the morning.

You pass a grocer's with local vegetables in the window.
You pass a baker's with new-made bread in the window.
You turn a corner to your right
and walk past a back garden with a low wall.

In the middle of the lawn,
a man is standing with wire mesh in his hand.
He is staring at a large box.
He wears a fawn jersey,
has close-cropped hair and a moustache.

He looks up, catches your eye and says, 'Hello.'
You return the compliment and,
looking towards the house, you say,
'Do you live here?'

He says no, he was just staying there last night.
You ask him what he is doing.

He turns the big box around, saying,

'Have you never seen one of these before?'

You recognize that it's a rabbit hutch.

'Is it yours?' you ask.
'No,' he says,
'it belongs to the wee* girl who lives here.
She was breaking her heart this morning.
The wind blew the hutch over last night
and the rabbit escaped.
She's found the rabbit
and now I'm mending the cage.'

'Are you keen on rabbits?' you ask.
'Not particularly,' he says.
'Are you keen on woodwork?' you ask.
'I used to be,' he replies.

> *(Pause)*

There's a silence, and you look at the man's face ...
He's a little embarrassed.
You look at his eyes: not blue or green – but brown eyes,
and though he's embarrassed, his eyes are smiling.
There's another silence.

> *(Pause)*

'Are you Jesus?'

And he says, 'Yes'.
And before you can help it, you ask,
'Then why, with all the things that need sorted in the world,
are you mending a rabbit hutch?'

He nods in the direction of the house and says,
'In there is a wee* girl who was breaking her heart this morning.
I asked her the one thing that I could do to make her happy
and she said, 'Would you mend my rabbit's hutch, Jesus?'
And who am I to refuse a child?'

Then he turns to you
and says, 'What's the one thing I can do to make you happy?'

* *or* little girl

And you tell him.
Now ... you tell him.

(Pause followed by a meditative song)

And now that you've told him,
you trust him.
And you leave him to get on mending the rabbit hutch
for the wee* girl,
knowing that when the time is right,
and even before it's right,
he'll attend to you.

PETHLA

Although this meditation requires the participants to imagine themselves visiting a hospital, its use is not restricted to services of healing. It is essentially about God's interest in each individual life.

It can be read by one person, but is best suited to two voices, in which case the principal reader says all the words in standard type, including phrases such as 'she says.' The second voice reads only the words in capitals.

The meditation is best led into, and out of, with quiet music.

You are in a hospital,
visiting a friend who is in a large general medical ward.

You have been in the ward several times and always,
as you leave, you look into a single room on the left-hand side,
just before the main ward door.

There is a woman lying there who is in a coma.
She is fed by a drip and never moves.
She is a brown woman ...
possibly Turkish or maybe Iranian,
but her skin is very dry
and has a sickly yellowish look about it.

You never stare at her, you just notice her.
You know she will always be there, always the same,
every time you leave your friend's bed
and walk down the ward towards the door.

That's the way she will be today ... just the same ...

But no ... as you look in, there is someone else in her room ...
a woman in a dark green coat with auburn hair.
You cannot see her face, you can only see her back
and a string bag with a book inside it,
which you notice has a brown paper jacket.
The bag is lying at the foot of the bed.

The visitor is sitting on the bed ...
she is taking the sick woman's hand in hers,
and she is saying something.

You move closer to the door
to hear a quiet voice saying one word repeatedly.

It does not seem to be an English word ...
it takes a while to make it out.
But gradually it becomes clear ... PETHLA ... PETHLA.

She says it again and again,
holding the sick woman's hand,
speaking very gently,
but very positively ... PETHLA ... PETHLA.

And as you look, the eyes of the sick woman open ...
for the first time in who knows how long ...
and she looks with disbelief at the stranger on her bed.
And you watch as visibly her dull skin changes colour ...
from a sickly yellow to a warm brown.
And now she begins to smile.
It is a tired but relieved smile.

The stranger bends forward,
kisses the sick woman on the brow
and gets up from the bed.

You stand back ... you don't want to let it be known
that you have been eavesdropping.

You turn to the side, but from the corner of your eye
you see the form of the visitor
with her dark green coat and auburn hair
walk out of the ward and along the corridor.

You wait a moment, then you decide to follow her.
You hurry along as she turns the corner.
Soon you are on her heels.

'Excuse me,' you say ... and she stops.

'YES?' – she says, gradually turning round.

'I've been watching you,' you say,
'I saw what happened.
I saw that sick woman open her eyes and smile.
What was it you did?'

And she replies –
'SHE JUST NEEDED TO KNOW THAT SHE WAS KNOWN.'

'I'm sorry,' you say.

'SHE JUST NEEDED TO KNOW THAT SHE WAS KNOWN.'

And, with that, the stranger puts her string bag on a bench.
She sits down and beckons you to kneel down in front of her.

You do ...

and on your head you feel her hands resting.

But this is something more,
more than the hands of a middle-aged woman,
more than gentle hands that touch and caress.
These hands were meant, somehow, to rest on your head.
You know this as your eyes close, not to darkness
but to bright pools of light –
red and gold and yellow and orange.

And then you hear her voice saying one word repeatedly.

But it is not the word you heard before.
It is not the word spoken over the sick woman.

This word ... is your name ...
                your name ...
spoken again and again and again,
deeply and gently and slowly.

        (Pause)

And in the voice of this unknown woman,
you sense the voice of time and eternity –
        the voice of the one
whose word is behind all words,
whose hand made every hand.

And gradually you sense –
you know in this instant –

that you are known,
that every hair of your head is numbered,
    every beat of your heart is intended,
    every hurt and every hope is recognized.

    (Pause)

Then there is a stillness,
in the midst of which you realize
that the voice has stopped and the hands have gone.
As you open your eyes, there is no sight of the stranger,
but where she sat there is the book wrapped in brown paper.

It has been left for you, open ...

open at a page headed 'Isaiah'.
These words are underlined:

> *Even if a mother should forget her child,*
> *I will never forget you.*
>
> *I have written your name*
> *on the palm of my hands.*

ON THE BUS

This is an extended meditation. Some people might call it a 'fantasy journey' in which their imagination is engaged. If the people with whom it is used have never shut their eyes for a meditation before, this is perhaps not the best one to begin with, as it may take up to 10 minutes to read.

It should not be accompanied by music, but it may be followed by music to allow the participants to come out of their imagined world into the worship setting again.

The meditation works best when read by two voices, though one sensitive voice can suffice. If a second voice is being used, it should preferably be that of a woman, reading the words in capitals. Words in square brackets are read only when one voice is leading the meditation.

You are sitting on a bus ...
an ordinary single decker bus going on an ordinary journey ...
to your home or to a friend's home.
There are only another three people in the bus:
a woman with two children, sitting near the front.
It is about four o'clock in the afternoon.
It's a dull day and this makes you glad to be in the warmth.

You are enjoying the journey, daydreaming,
looking out of the window,
not being disturbed by anyone or anything.

The bus stops and out get the mother and two children.
The bus waits, then on comes an old woman,
not very tall, but quite stout,
wearing an old brown coat, and a cheap green head square.
In her arms she is carrying a bundle of something or other.
You can't quite see it, until she pays her fare
and comes up the bus,
intending to sit across the passage from you.
You look at her closely as she makes to sit down ...

her brown coat,
her cheap green head square with a rose pattern on the borders.
She is quite stout and she has straggly grey hair
which falls across her brow.
And under her arm she carries a bundle of newspapers ...
evening newspapers.

She looks around, and sees you staring at her.

'HELLO,' ... [she says]
... and you say hello back.

As you look at her you see that she has a round face,
weather beaten ... with two small piercing blue eyes ...
but a smiling face ... made comical because when she speaks,
you see that her top front tooth is missing.

She keeps looking at you, smiling.

You feel you should say something ...
but you don't know what ....
Then you nod at the bunch of newspapers under her arm
and, assuming her to be a street vendor, you say,
'Is that your full time job?'

'OH NO, THIS IS JUST A VERY SMALL PART OF MY JOB,' [she says.]

'So, what do you do?' [you ask ... and she smiles.]
'I mean ... what are you?' [you ask ... and she smiles.]

'I'M AN ANGEL,' [she replies.]

And you feel you want to snigger.
You turn your head away to look out of the window
and then you turn it back and say quickly, 'You're a what?'

'I'M AN ANGEL,' [she says.]

'No you're not!'

'HAVE YOU SEEN AN ANGEL BEFORE?' [she asks.]

'No ... but ...'

'NO ... BUT ...

YOU HAVEN'T SEEN AN ANGEL BEFORE.

SO YOU WOULDN'T KNOW ONE IF YOU SAW ONE.

SOMETIMES ANGELS GET DRESSED UP AS WRESTLERS,

WITH SWEAT BANDS ON THEIR WRISTS.

SOMETIMES THEY GET DRESSED UP LIKE BUILDING SURVEYORS,

AND CARRY PLUMB LINES IN THEIR HANDS.

AND SOMETIMES THEY APPEAR LIKE OLD NEWSPAPER SELLERS,

WITH GREY HAIR AND TEETH MISSING.

WE DON'T ALWAYS WEAR WINGS AND HALOES, YOU KNOW.'

You can hardly speak ... but then you ask,
'What are you doing here?'

'I'M DOING WHAT ANGELS NORMALLY DO,' [she replies,]
'I'M BRINGING A MESSAGE.'

'Who for?' [you ask]

'FOR YOU.'

'For me? ... but who from?'

'FROM GOD.'

And while you stare in total disbelief,
the old woman puts her hand into her brown coat pocket
and brings out a blue envelope.

'IS THIS YOUR NAME?' [she asks,]
and she shows you the envelope
on which you see your name written ...
your first name ... in clear handwriting.

'Yes,' [you answer.]

'THEN IT'S FOR YOU.'

'What's it about?' [you ask, and she says,]

'IT'S THE ONE THING YOU ALWAYS FORGET,
AND THE ONE THING YOU'LL NEED TO REMEMBER
IF YOU ARE GOING TO GET ANYWHERE IN LIFE.'

'Pardon?'

'IT'S THE ONE THING YOU ALWAYS FORGET,
AND THE ONE THING YOU'LL NEED TO REMEMBER
IF YOU ARE GOING TO GET ANYWHERE IN LIFE.'

'Do you know what it says?' [you ask.]

'YES ... AND MAYBE SO DO YOU.'

Then she stretches out her hand
and gives you the blue envelope
with your name on the front.
You accept it and look at it in total confusion.
You want to pinch yourself to make sure that it's true.

You look up again at the old woman.
But she's not there.
The bus hasn't stopped, it's still moving,
but she's not there.
So you've been having a daydream ...
and then you look at your hand ...
and there is still the blue envelope with your name ...
and in it a message from God ...
something that you always forget.
And you begin to wonder what it might be.

What is it you always forget?
Has it to do with your prayers?
Has it to do with the church?
Has it to do with the person you keep criticizing?
Has it to do with some habit you know you have to kick?
What is it you always forget?

> *(Pause)*

You begin to get scared ...
your hands shake a bit ...
if God knows everything ...
then what is written inside might be quite devastating.

You look at the envelope again ...
and you tug at the corner until it opens ...

you put your finger inside and take out a card ... a white card.
The side you look at has nothing on it.
The message must be on the other side ...
the thing you always forget,
the thing you need to remember ...

You turn the card over.
There are four words in clear handwriting.

'I, God, love <u>you</u>.'

Is this what you forget ... is this what you have to remember?

You look again.

'I, God, love <u>you</u>.'

... and the '<u>you</u>' is underlined.

THE CUPBOARD

Like 'On the Bus', this is an extended meditation and may take up to 20 minutes. It is important that the reader should feel for the listeners' need to pause and think.

The meditation will not be suitable for every gathering of people. It was originally intended for a group of very busy church workers who were reflecting on their concerns at a conference.

It does not have a musical interlude, but may be followed by music leading to a hymn or song. If you are tempted to follow the meditation with a prayer, think twice. Participants may have shared with God something that another person's prayer might belittle or fail to encompass.

Think of the cupboard.

It is in the corner of your house
and you have not opened it for a long time.

Picture it.

The paintwork is old, the handle is dusty.
You stand facing it,
trying to remember what is behind the door,
but not quite sure ...
   is it books from the past,
   or old files or old clothes,
   or the things left over from childhood,
   or glass jars and rolls of wallpaper
   kept in a safe place but never needed?

Because you cannot quite remember,
and because there is time,
you stretch out and touch the handle.
You open the door.

The smell of mustiness meets you instantly.
That's the smell you expected ... but the sight is different.

The shelves are neatly stacked,

stacked with cardboard boxes ... the size of shoeboxes ...
and all are in attractive colours –
scarlet and orange
and apple green and turquoise,
lilac and bronze
and deep yellow and silver grey.
Such attractive boxes ... and each one has a white label ...
some have writing on them ... others have not.

You look at the labels
... and read the words printed on some of them:

MAJOR DISAPPOINTMENTS ... says one,

BROKEN PROMISES ... says another.

LOST LOVES

UNRESOLVED CONFLICTS

NAGGING DOUBTS

BIGGEST FAILURES

There are more yet as you move your eyes along ...

ANGER

NO ENCOURAGEMENT

NO THANKS

UNANSWERED PRAYERS

SECRET WISHES

Perhaps there are 30 boxes in all ...
and perhaps 20 or 25 have names on white labels.

But some labels are blank.
You see resting on the shelf
a black ink marker and you wonder ...
You wonder should you?
Then you decide to write some other categories
on the blank labels.

What will you write?
What words will ring bells about who has failed you
or what you fear or what annoys you?

You write ... what do you write? ...

PERSONAL HIT-LIST
CHIEF REGRET
AWKWARD CUSTOMERS

... or what? What do you write?

(Pause)

You stand back and you look again at the boxes,
at the labels you noticed earlier:

MAJOR DISAPPOINTMENTS
BROKEN PROMISES
LOST LOVES
UNRESOLVED CONFLICTS
NAGGING DOUBTS
ANGER
NO ENCOURAGEMENT
NO THANKS
SECRET WISHES.

And the labels which you wrote yourself ...

(Pause)

You look at them and sense a weird attractiveness in it all.

Maybe these boxes could be of some use ...
maybe letters could be filed in them ...
maybe slips of paper ... names, could be put in them ...
maybe ... maybe ...

You lift one of the boxes, a scarlet one ...
it's empty and it's light.
You reckon you could perhaps take eight or nine in your arms.
So you choose which ones you'll take.

You look again at the labels facing you
and you choose the ones you want to take.

(Pause)

You pile them on your arms ... the labels facing you ...

they come up to your chin ... and a bit above ...
you balance the boxes
and with your foot you shut the cupboard.
And you're just thinking
about where to put your new discoveries
when the front door bell rings.

Who could it be?

You go to the window and look outside ...
three houses along, nuns are collecting money for charity ...
but you can't see if it is a nun at your door.
You can't see the door.

The door bell rings again.

You go to another window ...
You peer round the boxes and see,
on the other side of the street,
a little girl crossing the road ... she's running fast ...
you see her trip ...
down she goes ...
and the tears start ...
and you want to help her ...
but you're holding these boxes ...
and there is someone at the door.

You begin to panic ...
where will you put them?
They're getting heavier now ...
awkward to carry.
You can't return them to the cupboard,
because you have shut it.
You can't put them in the hall or in the sitting room ...
What would anyone think if they saw these titles
which so attracted you earlier?

The door bell rings again ...
and you feel you have to answer it ...
it might be important ...

So, in a sweat you make your way to the door,
watching your feet in case you stumble.
As you get to it, the bell rings again.
Almost in desperation you say ... 'It's open!'
The handle turns and the door swings towards you.

But who is standing there you can't see ...
because the boxes are between you and the stranger.
And just as you feel you are going to panic,
a warm, reassuring voice says,
'I've come to take your boxes away'.

Then two hands touch yours and relieve you of your burden.
And you see going away from you
the things you were so keen to clutch not so long ago ...
you watch them move away from you ...
the attractive boxes ...
with the curiously attractive titles ...

THE DISAPPOINTMENTS,

THE LETDOWNS,

THE HIT-LIST,

THE POOR-ME'S,

THE CHIEF REGRETS YOU HAVE ALMOST COME TO CHERISH.

(Pause)

You do not see the face of the stranger
who has relieved you of your load ...
you only see the back.

You stare as the stranger walks down the street
and into the distance
and you would stare longer ...
but something is pulling at your leg.

You look down ...
and there on the doorstep is the little girl
with the skinned knee.

You can help her now ...
Your hands are free.

WRITING IT DOWN

Sometimes people experience difficulty when there is a silence in worship. The reasons are understandable, most immediate of which is that few people, in their daily lives, experience or are aware of silence.

In this meditation, silence should not be a problem, as there is a focus on which participants can set their minds. People should be asked to close their eyes and the reader should speak slowly, pausing now and then where appropriate.

Depending on the group, the reader may wish to repeat the things which people might want, in imagination, to write down. Or it may seem best just to mention these once and let silence follow.

It is helpful to have a solo voice sing a song of penitence in the middle of the meditation. It should be unaccompanied to save fuss with instruments. Alternatively a meditative song may be sung by all.

SUITABLE SONG (SEE PAGE 104)
KYRIE ELEISON (GHANA)

Picture yourself at a table or at a desk ... one you know,
the one at which you would sit in order to write a letter.

Picture a piece of paper before you ...
the kind of paper you normally write on and a pen,
the kind of pen you normally use.

And prepare to write ... not a letter, not a note,
but some names, some words, some short words ... to God.

Picture yourself writing to God,
writing down the things you so often keep back,
in case they offend God or embarrass you.

You may want to write of ...

the pain that has not gone away;
the prayer that has not been answered;
the person who hopes you will fail, not succeed;

the part of you that has not fallen into place;
the part of God for which you can find no place.

Write it down ... a word ... a phrase ... a name ... a plea.

(Here the above list may be repeated then a
silence follows.)

And now picture yourself folding the paper in half
and folding it again and looking for an envelope,
but seeing a hand, a kindly hand,
which does not scare or threaten.

You look no further than the hand,
for it is God's hand
and there is no need to see God's face.

You give God the note
of all you have kept back,
of what makes you despair in the silent corners of your soul.

(Here a song may be sung solo or together.)

You stare at your desk, at your table,
where the paper was,
and look – it has come back again,
folded as before.

You open it gradually,
enough to see that what was there
is there no longer.

Instead, in another hand, the word ... 'Thanks.'

It is signed ... 'God'.

It has a PS ... 'I mean it.'

THE SAINTS OF GOD

Like 'The Testimony and Prayers of Three Anonymous Children', this is both reflective and devotional. It was originally prepared for use in a small group on All Saints Day. But there is no mention of the type of people after whom churches have been named.

Here, the worshippers are enabled to remember and give thanks to God for humble rather than high folk who, at various stages in their lives, have shaped, nourished or shown them faith.

The meditation needs a focal area – a table (or other raised area) that all can see – where four objects representing different stages of life will be brought and set down. General low lighting, if it is possible, would be helpful but the objects on the table must be well lit so that each can be seen clearly from the furthest seat. Participants will be distracted if their view is obstructed, so work out the sightlines in advance and set markers for the objects. Next to each marker should be a large candle, already lit. Allow space for participants to put small candles or paper symbols by each object at the end of the meditation. The four objects suggested are:

BABYHOOD:	*a nappy, folded and pinned*
CHILDHOOD:	*an evidently old teddy bear*
ADOLESCENCE:	*a school tie*
ADULTHOOD:	*a batch of keys.*

Lest some people feel that the meditation may be too 'secular', it may be helpful to have a large cross in the middle of the table.

After the final meditative words have been read, the worship leader may suggest that if people wish to thank God for someone brought to mind, they may do so by lighting a small candle and placing it next to the appropriate object, as the response is sung repeatedly. Alternatively – as was the original action – everyone may be given one or two cut-out triangles (which can be photocopied from the appendix). The sign of three circles so arranged in a triangle is an ancient Celtic symbol for a saint, sometimes put on the sleeve or skirt of a figure in an ancient manuscript to indicate their sanctity.

After the activity, the leader may conclude with the prayer suggested here or another.

Please note that the section headings, e.g. BABYHOOD, should not be read aloud.

SUITABLE SONG (SEE PAGE 104)
UBI CARITAS ET AMOR (TAIZÉ)

(B A B Y H O O D)

READER A: Lord, you created every part of me;
you put me together in my mother's womb.
When my bones were being formed,
when I was growing there in secret,
you knew that I was there.
You saw me before I was born.   *(from Psalm 139)*

*(READER B brings the nappy to the table and
sets it down, then returns to his/her place.)*

READER B: Before I was born,
you prayed for me;
and when I moved from the womb into the world,
your arms cradled me;
and you sang your funny songs
and you made sense of my wordless language;
and you held my hand
till I slept,
till I walked,
till I lost my fear,
till I was old enough to let your hand go.

(Sung response)

(C H I L D H O O D)

READER A: We will not keep back from our children,
we will tell the next generation

about the Lord's power and his great deeds
and the wonderful things God has done.

For God instructed our ancestors
to teach his laws to their children,
so that the next generation might learn from them
and in turn should tell their children. *(from Psalm 78)*

(READER C brings the teddy bear to the table,
sets it down, then returns to his/her place.)

READER C: When I was a child,
you prayed for me;
when I broke my heart or bruised my skin,
you cared for me;
when I was keen to learn,
you taught me.
You watched my eyes bulge
with the wonder of the world;
you heard me repeat you,
you let me cheat you;
and sometimes you stopped me
from doing what I wanted.

Even today,
I am restrained and enriched
by what you did then.

(Sung response)

(A D O L E S C E N C E)

READER A: Teach me your ways, O Lord;
make them known to me.
Teach me to live according to your truth,
for you are my God, who saves me.
I always trust in you.

Remember, O Lord, your kindness and constant love
which you have shown from long ago.

Forgive the sins and errors of my youth.
In your constant love and goodness remember me.

(from Psalm 25)

*(READER D brings the tie to the table, sets it
down, then returns to his/her place.)*

READER D: When I left childhood
you prayed for me;
when I was silent with my parents,
I spoke to you;
when I felt awkward with my body,
I trusted you.
And though you gave me good advice,
sometimes I ignored it;
and though you gave me my liberty,
sometimes I abused it;
and though you spoke of God,
sometimes I did not want to know.

You held me through the difficult years,
and I reap the benefit now.

(Sung response)

(A D U L T H O O D)

READER A: You, Lord, have taught me ever since I was young;
now that I am old and my hair is grey,
do not abandon me.

Your righteousness, O God, reaches the skies.
You have done great things;
there is no one like you.

You have sent troubles and suffering on me,
but you will restore my strength;
you will keep me from the grave.
You will make me greater than ever;
you will comfort me again.   *(from Psalm 71)*

49

*(READER E brings the keys to the table, sets
them down, then returns to his/her place.)*

READER E: Since I have become the adult I longed to be,
you've prayed for me.
When I've had to cope with failure,
you accepted me;
when I have doubted my abilities,
you've encouraged me;
when I've met with some success,
you've smiled at me without envy.

And when the church has become an irrelevance
and my faith has run low,
you've let God touch me.

(Sung response)

*(After silence, worshippers may be invited to
light a candle, or lay a symbol or write a note
near whichever symbol has been particularly
evocative of a person in their past who
nourished their faith. As they do this the
response is sung again repeatedly. The
following prayer may be used in conclusion.)*

PRAYER: Thank you, Lord,
for Moses and Miriam,
for Sarah and Abraham,
for Peter and Martha,
for Mary and Paul
and for all the other Bible people
from whose lives we learn.

And thank you
for your other saints:
the ones perhaps known only to us
who never made headline news on earth,
but whose faith and love,

trust and commitment,
have made headline news in heaven.

Having around us this cloud of witnesses –
these mothers and fathers,
brothers and sisters in God –
may we honour their influence
by following him
whose footsteps they followed,
wearing our own shoes.
AMEN.

*B*iblical

WHEN THE TIME WAS RIGHT

The creation story in Genesis 1 appears in the form of a poem or hymn with a refrain at the conclusion of the events of each day. That style is imitated in this poem which was originally meant for use by children.

Different readers may take a verse while others act out or symbolize the events being referred to.

1. God looked into space
   but nothing was around:
   just darkness and wind,
   not a smell, sight or sound.
   Then God said to himself,
   'I think we'll have light.'
   So the darkness stopped
   when the time was right.

2. God made night and day,
   but they weren't the same.
   Then he made sea and sky
   and he gave each its name;
   and when God saw the ocean
   which was sparkling and bright,
   he was glad he'd made water
   when the time was right.

3. God said to himself,
   'Now I'd like to see land.
   I'd like meadows and mountains
   and shores full of sand.'
   So he brought earth from water
   and was pleased with the sight
   of the plants which all grew
   when the time was right.

4. Then God looked at the sky
   and he found it too plain.
   It was all coloured blue
   and was filled up with rain.
   So he made sun and moon
   to change day into night
   and the stars blinked their eyes
   when the time was right.

5. God looked at the land
   and decided, one day,
   to put fish in the sea
   and make sure that they'd stay.
   He put birds in the air
   and they all shook with fright
   till God taught them to fly
   when the time was right.

6. Then God made the animals,
   some small and some large,
   and soon he was asking
   'Who on earth will take charge?'
   So he waited and wondered,
   till with careful insight
   he made man and made woman
   when the time was right.

7. Then God watched from a distance
   to see what they'd do
   with the world and its creatures
   and with each other too.

   Sometimes they forgot
   what God wanted or said.
   Then they'd go their own way

and do their will instead.
And it hurt God that people,
who he'd made out of love,
should forget how to live,
what to say, where to move.

Should he punish and hate them?
Should he leave them to fight?
No. He sent to them Jesus
when the time was right.

8.   Today we enjoy
all that God's love has done
and thank him for our world,
for our lives, for his Son;
and we sing songs of praise
to express our delight
at all God meant to be
when the time was right.

ON THE EIGHTH DAY

The concern for the environment which has emerged as a prime preoccupation is not a concern alien to biblical faith. The tragedy is that despite having a mandate in the second chapter of Genesis to be stewards of the earth, Christians have put that low in their list of priorities.

This meditation is almost a litany of the undoing of creation. It does not end on a happy note, but on a question which a sensitive worship leader might wish to use as a lead into prayer or into an act of corporate repentance.

The script allows for a variety of expression. The two readers should be positioned apart from each other, and God, rather than being located centrally, might speak from behind the congregation. Ideally, a screen between the two readers might be used to show pictures of the various types of destruction alluded to in the text.

Alternatively, lights could be extinguished at the end of each day as the response is sung.

SUITABLE SONGS (SEE PAGE 104)
KYRIE ELEISON (GHANA)

READER A: After the making of heaven and earth,
and after the time of resting;
and after the Word had returned from the flesh,
and after the Spirit's sending,
God gazed, in love, over creation.
And, behold,
the world had lost its intended form
and thick darkness brooded everywhere.

ALL: *(Sung response)*

READER B: On the eighth day,
God looked on humanity;
and humanity was in a mess.
Emaciated by hunger,
bloated by excess,

maimed by war,
blinded by bigotry,
the people of earth lurched towards the abyss.
Women, demeaned and exploited,
Men, turned brute by their basest desires,
no longer bore their Creator's image.
And God said,

GOD: Do they not remember
how I lifted them like children to my cheek?
Have they now forgotten
that I have written their name on my hands?
This is not good.
I call on the evening and I call on the morning
to witness my displeasure.
And I long for a different day.

ALL: *(Sung response)*

READER A: On the ninth day,
God looked at the creatures of earth;
and the creatures of earth were in a mess.
The fish of the sea were bloated with cancers,
the birds of the air were swaddled in oil,
the beasts of the wild were hunted as trophies,
the beasts of the field were imprisoned in factories;
animals everywhere fell prey to experiment,
tortured and tested behind the smokescreen of science.
And God said,

GOD: What shall become of the humble donkey,
the gentle beast which carried my son?
What shall become of the graceful swallow
which built its nest in the eaves of my house?
This is not good.
I call on the evening and I call on the morning
to witness my displeasure.
And I long for a different day.

ALL: *(Sung response)*

READER B: On the tenth day,
God looked at the sky,
and the sky was in a mess.
The sun, once earth's friend,
had become a great danger,
threatening the world
through a peppered ozone layer;
the stars which once spoke
of the harmony of heaven,
now witnessed with horror
the militarization of the galaxy.
And God said,

GOD: Does humankind no longer
lift up its eyes and wonder?
Must earth destroy the tapestry
my hands are still embroidering?
This is not good.
I call on the evening and I call on the morning
to witness my displeasure.
And I long for a different day.

ALL: *(Sung response)*

READER A: On the eleventh day,
God looked at the fertile earth,
and the fertile earth was in a mess.
Fields which should have fed the hungry
grew cash crops for 'civilized' cravings;
pastures had become barren
through constant overgrazing;
rainforests had vanished
to pay off debt and interest;
fruit and grain were suspect
where prone to overspraying;
trees were scabbed and wilted
through lack of healthy air.
And God said,

GOD: Where are the lilies of the field,
arrayed in majestic splendour?
How safe are the ears of corn
my Son once picked on a Sabbath?
This is not good.
I call on the evening and I call on the morning
to witness my displeasure.
And I long for a different day.

ALL: *(Sung response)*

READER B: On the twelfth day,
God looked at the land and sea,
and the land and sea were in a mess.
Contaminated by waste, debilitated by detergents,
the gentle waves heaved with hideous terror;
the ground, fouled with fertilizer,
had lost its inherent goodness;
and, tainted by nuclear fall-out,
deserts glistened with living death.
And God said,

GOD: How can the valleys sing with joy?
How can the seas roar in triumph?
How can the mountains clap their hands
if nature is bereaved?
This is not good.
I call on the evening and I call on the morning
to witness my displeasure.
And I long for a different day.

ALL: *(Sung response)*

READER A: On the thirteenth day,
God looked at light and darkness,
and light and darkness were in a mess.
Truth was in exile,
displaced by lies and rumour.
Imperialism masqueraded as justice;
intervention wore the cloak of welfare;

cheap pleasure stole the mantle of love,
and the religion of the privileged
was proclaimed heir to the throne
of the Saviour of the poor.
And God said,

GOD: Who can believe what I have seen?
To whom did I think
I had revealed my power?
This is not good.
I call on the evening and I call on the morning
to witness my displeasure.
And I long for a different day.

ALL: *(Sung response)*

READER B: On the fourteenth day,
God looked away from the world
which was born out of love
and crafted with beauty.
And God wept.

ALL: *(Sung response)*

READER A: When the time of the weeping was done,
God said,

GOD: I have kept faith with my children on earth.
I have trusted them
to be stewards of the land
and guardians of its creatures.
I promised them nature's kindly gifts
as long as they lived with justice.
I promised them every spiritual gift
as long as they cared for creation.
And then,
then when I saw they had lost their way
and lived and languished far from me,
I sent my Son to save the world
and bring my people home.

ALL: *(Sung response)*

GOD: Oh, children of earth,
       you have witnessed my love.
       Do you now want to witness my anger?
       In silence I will wait.
       I will watch and I will wait.

       Choose now, my sons and daughters,
       what shall brood over you –
       thick darkness
       or the Holy Spirit?

MEETING GOD

If some of the characters in the Bible were to give their testimony, as at an evangelical rally, the audience might well stare in disbelief. In this meditation, four biblical characters tell of how, not on the Sabbath, but at other times, they were confronted with their Maker.

These cameo testimonies could be used to spark off discussion or, if used in a worship context and interspersed with a sung response, they can be followed by the prayer given here.

The latter use may be enhanced by having the four people come to the centre of the worship area and speak as if they were giving a testimony, perhaps lighting a candle before they return to their seats.

SUITABLE SONGS (SEE PAGE 104)

BE STILL AND KNOW (WGRG, IONA COMMUNITY)

BLESS THE LORD MY SOUL (TAIZÉ)

SANTO / HOLY, HOLY, HOLY (ARGENTINA)

JACOB: I met God on a Monday night ...
          and it was very disturbing.

          I'm not a violent man,
          I don't even argue much,
          but I felt like a fight that night.

          I had lain awake, a thousand things on my mind.
          And when, long after midnight,
          there was a knock at the door,
          I was up and downstairs like a bear with a sore paw.

          A stranger, standing there, stretched out his hand.
          I took it, out of anger more than friendship ...
          and he didn't let go.

          He didn't let go,
          so I started to tug,
          to pull away,
          to push him,
          to wrestle.

We wrestled till daybreak,
he never letting go,
until finally he said I had won ...

and that I had met God ...
wrestling.

(Sung response)

MOSES: I met God on a Tuesday afternoon ...
and it was very disturbing.

I was just doing my job
the way I always do my job.

I'm not ... or I wasn't ... a public person.

I didn't like talking to people
because I had a speech defect ... I stammered.

So, because of that,
and because of my past
which I don't want to go into,
I looked after animals ... sheep mostly.

I was just doing my job,
just minding my sheep,
just looking at the same grass,
the same hills I had looked at every day,

when I noticed a tree ...
an ordinary tree.

And suddenly, the ordinary became special:
the leaves became candles,
the dull earth became holy ground ...

and that's where I met God ...
when the ordinary became special.

(Sung response)

ELI: I met God on a Wednesday evening ...
and it was very disturbing.

I was tidying up the church
and I saw a woman sitting in the back corner,
next to the door.

I had seen her before.
She was what we ministers call a 'problem case' ...
she wore her problem all the time, everywhere ...
never smiled, always looked neurotic.

Her problem, mind you, wasn't easy to deal with.
She was childless,
and her husband had got in tow with another woman,
and had children by her.

Sometimes she wanted to talk about it.
Sometimes she sat by herself and cried or moped.

But this Wednesday, she looked drunk.

Her lips kept moving
and she seemed to be mumbling
like an alcoholic would do
after a night on the wine.

I said to her, 'Stop making a show of yourself!
Sober up, for goodness' sake.'

And then she looked at me,
and, perfectly calmly, said that
she hadn't been drinking ...
she had been praying.

I was quite embarrassed ...
So I said, 'I hope God gives you what you want.'

A month later she told me she was pregnant
and, thinking back,
I realized that I had met God
in the eyes of what seemed like a drunken woman.

(Sung response)

ELIJAH: I met God on a Thursday night
and it was very disturbing.

I had just won a competition,
and I felt totally depressed.

It wasn't a hollow victory ...
you might say it was divinely inspired,
but I felt depressed.

So I went for a walk into the hills,
where I felt I could be nearer to my Maker.

It was very beautiful, looking round about,
but I didn't feel a bit closer to him.

Then the wind got up,
and the ground started to shake.
I thought it was the end of the world.
I thought I'd see my Maker face to face before long.
But the wind dropped,
the shaking stopped and nothing happened.

Then, from nowhere it seemed, a fire started
and I remembered a story
about how someone first met God
when faced with fire.
But that didn't work for me.

It was afterwards ...
after the wind and the shaking and the fire ...
it was when I thought God had given up on me
that I met him ...
in silence.

(Sung response)

PRAYER: We bless you
that you are a God of many faces,
and the Bible is your picture book,
and your people are witnesses
to your amazing grace.

We bless you
that you are unpredictable.

We cannot say, 'Now God will appear,
now God will do this or do that.'

We can only say 'God is God
and God will surprise us.'

We bless you
that we are your children
who realize that we know you a little,
and not your contemporaries
who imagine that they know it all.

We bless you
and ask you to bless us
through peculiar kinds of people
in unexpected places,
just as you blessed
Jacob and Moses,
Sarah and Hannah,
Samuel and Elijah,
and all your saints.

AMEN.

HE WAS IN THE WORLD

This is a simple reflection on the life of Jesus. It does nothing more than highlight aspects of his life and ministry in and for the world.

Four readers are required who should speak as if telling a story. An appropriate song or piece of music should precede and follow the sections.

SUITABLE SONGS (SEE PAGE 104)

HE BECAME POOR (WGRG, IONA COMMUNITY)

BEHOLD THE LAMB OF GOD (WGRG, IONA COMMUNITY)

(Song or music)

READER A: He was in the world,
but the world, though it owed its being to him,
did not know him.
He came to his own,
but his own would not receive him.

Yet to all who did receive him,
to those who gave him their allegiance,
he gave the right to become children of God.

So the Word became flesh, and lived ... among ... us.

(Song or music)

READER B: He took five loaves and two fish,
and blessed and broke them
and fed the crowd.
And no-one understood,
but all forgot their hunger.

He spat on clay to moisten it
and rubbed the mixture on the eyes of a blind man.
And no-one understood,
but the man began to see.

He lay asleep in the midst of a storm
and, when wakened,

told the wind and waves to be quiet.
And no-one understood,
but all became calm again.

(Song or music)

READER C: He was in the line of the prophets.
He was able to meet with the great.
He knew people of knowledge and intellect.

But when it came to showing
who was the greatest in the kingdom of heaven,
he did not take a ruler or a wise man
or a religious guru.

He put a toddler in the middle and said,
'Unless you become like a child,
you'll never enter the kingdom of heaven.'

(Song or music)

READER D: He called people to follow him,
to leave self behind and to go with him,
to take up their cross,
and to keep in step
with him who carries the weight of the world.

'Whoever cares for his own safety is lost,' he said.
'Whoever loves husband, wife, parent or child
more than me
is not worthy of me,' he said.

'Whoever loses herself for my sake,
will find her true self.' he said.

(Song or music)

READER A: He came to his own,
but his own would not receive him.
Yet to those who do receive him,
to those who give him their allegiance,
he gives the right
to become sons and daughters of the living God.

(Song or music)

BEHOLD THE LAMB OF GOD

More often than not, the title of this meditation, which is a quotation from John's Gospel, is associated with the death of Jesus. But it was not the cross which John pointed to when he uttered these words; it was a stranger standing in a crowd.

Here we simply take four different pictures of Jesus and allow John's words to be associated with them, in order to feel that these words were true for the whole of Jesus' life and not just for its ending.

The principle reader (A) may be located in view of the congregation. The others should be on the periphery.

The sung response is essential for this meditation.

SUITABLE SONG (SEE PAGE 104)
BEHOLD THE LAMB OF GOD (WGRG, IONA COMMUNITY)

> *(Sung response)*

READER A: He is watched by shepherds.
He is lying in wool;
he is gurgling, laughing, crying,
wetting himself,
wearying his mother.
It is a very old man who recognizes
the very young baby –

READER B: This child has been chosen by God
for the destruction of some
and the salvation of many.

> *(Sung response)*

READER A: He is speaking in the synagogue.
He is preaching from the prophets;
he is, discovering how his words
do not please religious people.

READER C: Who does he think he is?

READER D: I think we've heard enough!

READER C: Let's show him the door!

READER D: Let's show him the hill!

(Sung response)

READER A: He is walking through the streets
which most decent folk avoid.
He is listening to the cries
of all those who go unheard –

READER B: Touch me, Jesus.

READER C: Heal me, Jesus.

READER D: Lord, let me see again.

READER B: Lord, make me well again.

READER E: Jesus, it's my child!

(Sung response)

READER A: He is confronting his fiercest critics.
They have tongues as sharp as razors.
They have plans
in case their tongues are not enough.

READER C: Why do you eat with the riff-raff?

READER D: Why do you call yourself God's son?

READER C: Why do you violate our traditions?

READER D: Why don't you take us seriously?

READER E: Judas? ... Judas? ... we've a job for you.

(Sung response)

READER A: This is him,   from Bethlehem to
Bethany,
                    from Jerusalem to Jericho,
                    from Capernaum to Calvary,
                    from Golgotha to the grave,
                    from heaven to hell and back again;

saying: 'I am the Way ... follow me.
I am the Truth ... believe me.
I am the Life ... receive me.'

(Sung response)

THE TESTIMONY AND PRAYER
OF THREE ANONYMOUS CHILDREN

Originally written for the European Conference of Christian Educators which met in Scotland in September 1989 this, as its title suggests, is both a reflection and a prayer.

The readers represent three anonymous children whom Jesus touched. They read as adults reflecting on the experience of their childhood, and asking to be like children again.

If this material is going to lead into prayer – which it can do very easily – every worshipper should have in his or her hand three small, individual pictures which can be photocopies of the illustrations in the appendix. Please note, it is important that they have three pieces of paper and not one A4 sheet with three diagrams. Some cutting up is required.

The leader of worship should indicate that, for this meditation, two things are required: firstly that we sing a verse song before and after its three sections; and secondly that we look at one picture at a time, beginning with (1).

It may be helpful for the leader to say that, as the meditation proceeds, there may be children known to the worshippers who come to mind. If so, they might like to write names down on the reverse of the appropriate picture.

There should be a cross centrally in the worship area. If prayer is to follow on from the meditation, let there be a short silence. Then the leader should suggest that if particular children have been brought to mind whose plight or potential people would like to lay before Jesus, they may do so, as the song resumes, by laying the appropriate picture with or without a name on the back around the cross. After the activity, the leader might say a short prayer offering the action of the worshippers to God.

SUITABLE SUNG RESPONSE (SEE PAGE 104)

YOUR KINGDOM COME, O LORD (RUSSIAN ORTHODOX)

(Sung response)

VOICE A *(male)*:

When I was a child,
I gave him all I had.

He stood among hungry people
who needed fed.
And I believed that he knew
how to make the food go round.

Now that I am an adult,
I have much more to share.
But, though the crowds are still hungry,
I am reluctant to give him what I have.

Lord, when today I see the face of those
who long for food and justice,
when I hear their cry,
make me as generous as when I was a child.

(Sung response)

VOICE B *(female)*:

When I was a child,
he told me to get up.

Outside my window, the neighbours were saying,
'She's a hopeless case. There's no help for her.'
But he put them to silence
and told me to get up.

Now that I am an adult,
sometimes doubt, sometimes frustration,
sometimes failure, sometimes sadness,
surround my bed;
and I hear the voices of those who criticize
more easily than I hear the voice of the one
who encourages.

Lord, when I hear the voices outside which condemn
and the voices inside which discourage,

make me as keen to listen to you
as when I was a child.

(Sung response)

VOICE C *(male or female)*:
When I was a child,
he put his hand on me.

Others wanted to keep me away,
believing he had better things to do.
But I pushed my way through the crowd,
and sat on his knee and let him touch me.

Now that I am an adult,
sometimes I think that he is too busy
and often I say that I am too busy
to let his hand rest on me.

Lord,
when so many excuses keep us apart
make me as keen to let you touch me
as when I was a child.

(Sung response)

LAZARUS

The account of the raising of Lazarus in John 11, is magnificent in its detail and in how it moves from what seems like numb acceptance on the part of Jesus to participative restoration.

This representation of the story is best used when people are sitting in a circle or semi-circle so that the five symbols which accompany the meditation can clearly be seen.

Four different voices represent the characters in the story. Each has his or her own symbol. But the Disciple, Martha and Mary should also have an unravelled bandage which, after the final section of the meditation they each place on the same spot.

It is suggested that these might be appropriate symbols:

SILENCE:	*a watch or clock*
SIGHT:	*a handkerchief*
SMELL:	*a bottle of ammonia*
SOUND:	*a microphone head*
ACTION:	*unravelled bandages*

Alternatively, copies of the illustrations in the appendix may be cut out and used.

This is especially helpful if a large group is divided into small groups. Whether there is one group or several, the narrative should be read by one set of readers in the hearing of all. At the appropriate times, the small group leader puts the symbol in the centre.

Each section is followed by the congregational verse or chant which begins the meditation.

It is very easy to move from reflecting on the story of Lazarus to prayer.

The worship leader need just mention simple categories after which people (if forewarned) should be able to mention a name or a situation. The sung response may be used again at the end of the prayer and, if wanted, candles may be lit next to the symbols. This will especially help those for whom an action would offer their prayer more easily than a word.

Please note that the section headings, e.g. THE SILENCE, *should not be read aloud.*

SUITABLE SUNG RESPONSES (SEE PAGE 104)
BLESS THE LORD, MY SOUL (TAIZÉ)
COME, HOLY SPIRIT (WGRG, IONA COMMUNITY)

(T H E   S I L E N C E)

READER A: A man named Lazarus, who lived in Bethany,
was ill.
His sisters, Martha and Mary,
sent a message to Jesus:
'Lord, your dear friend is ill.'
When Jesus heard the news,
he stayed where he was for two more days.

Then on the way to Bethany, he told his disciples,
'Our friend Lazarus has fallen asleep,
but I will go and wake him.'
They answered, 'But if he is asleep,
he will get well.'
Jesus responded that he meant that Lazarus had died.

DISCIPLE: Lord, your friend Lazarus is ill.

*(Sung response during which the first symbol
is placed centrally.)*

READER B: For two days he waited,
watched and waited,
till the worst had happened
and death had won.

Two days, still and silent,
until it was time to speak.
But he did not speak
before, in silence,
he knew the time was right.

(Silence)

(T H E   S I G H T)

READER A: As Jesus came to the village, first Mary
and then Martha came out to meet him.
When Mary arrived, she fell at his feet and said,
'Lord if you had been here,
my brother would not have died.'

Jesus saw her weeping
and he saw the other people with her weeping.
His heart was touched and he was deeply moved.
'Where have they buried him?' he asked them.

'Come and see, Lord,' they answered.

Jesus wept.

'See how he loved him,' some people said,
while others said,
'He gave sight to the blind, didn't he?
Could he not have kept this man from dying?'

MARY: 'Lord, if you had been there,
my brother would not have died!'

*(Sung response during which the second
symbol is placed centrally.)*

READER B: The Son of God has tears on his face –
in front of men who don't know how to cry,
in front of women who have grown tired of weeping.

Where is his composure now?
Where does his resistance lie?
God has made him weak enough,
and strong enough to cry.

(Silence)

(T H E   S M E L L)

READER A: Deeply moved once more,

Jesus went to the tomb which was a cave
with a stone
placed at the entrance.

'Take the stone away!' Jesus ordered.

Martha, the dead man's sister, said,
'There will be a stink, Lord.
He has been buried for four days!'

MARTHA: Lord, there will be a stink.
He has been buried for four days.

*(Sung response during which the third symbol
is placed centrally.)*

READER B: Death stinks.
So do cancer patients, sometimes.
So do scandals,
beggars,
boozers,
and see-through alibis.

We smell a rat and avoid getting contaminated.
Jesus kisses the lepers
and has a nose for recovery,
even when our heads are turned away.

(Silence)

(T H E   S O U N D)

READER A: They took the stone away.
Jesus prayed to God, then called out in a loud voice,
'Lazarus, come out!'

JESUS: Lazarus, come out!

*(Sung response during which the fourth
symbol is placed centrally.)*

READER B: A whisper to a corpse
is like a raindrop to a river.

When hope and love and life have gone,
the Son of God declines to moan or whisper.
He needs to shout:
'Lynn, Laura, Lazarus ... come out!'

(Silence)

(T H E   A C T I O N)

READER A: He came out,
his hands and feet wrapped in grave clothes,
and with a cloth round his face.
'Untie him,' said Jesus, 'and let him go.'

JESUS: Untie him! Let him go!

*(Sung response during which the fifth symbol
is placed centrally.)*

READER B: Dead men do not button their shrouds:
other hands must dress them.
So, commanded by Christ,
these 'other hands' must also untie
all whom their words or deeds have bound,
all whom their gossip has destroyed,
all whom their stares and stubbornness
have consigned to silence.

(Silence)

PRAYER: Let us mention before God:
those in whose lives
there is a silent time of waiting;

(Names may be said aloud)

those in whose lives
or for whose lives tears have been shed;

(Names may be said aloud)

those around whom
there is a stink of rumour, threat or danger;

(Names may be said aloud)

those who need to hear not a whisper
but a shout in the depth of their souls;

(Names may be said aloud)

those whom we, or others,
need to untie or liberate by word or action.

(Names may be said aloud)

THE TREE

The story of Jesus cursing the fruit tree is one of the more obscure in the Gospels, until we realize that God expects fruit from his followers in and out of season.

When this meditation was first used, people had been asked to draw a tree and talk to each other about what they had drawn and why. The drawings were then gathered in and, during Jesus' words of cursing, as people had their eyes shut, there was a sound of paper being torn, which the participants took to be their fondly drawn trees. In fact, scrap paper was employed, but the feeling that something that belonged to them was being destroyed, added to the poignancy of the meditation.

It is not advised that this practice happen in every situation. If it is done there should be a time of corporate reflection after the meditation which is not necessary if it is simply read as written.

The reading should be followed by music or a chant and people should be encouraged to close their eyes and use their imaginations to picture the happenings. The two readers should be located in different parts of the worship area.

READER: Imagine yourself as a tree ...
standing at a crossroads
where two country lanes meet;
standing up a bit, back a bit from the road,
with a view of the surrounding countryside;
standing in the warmest of days ...
warm, but not scorching,
warm enough to make you feel
at one with the world,
and glad to be where you are.

Feel for your roots ...
buried deep below you,
toes which you can't wiggle,
but which you know are there ...
deep, deep in the warm, moist earth.

Feel for your bark ...
showing the signs of age,
but not cruelly;
a bark which can tell stories
like an old woman's weather-beaten face.

Feel for your branches ... stretching out
like arms and fingers,
resting places for the birds,
sheltering places for travellers caught in a storm.

Feel for your leaves ...
fluttering in the gentle breeze,
fully grown, green and full of life.

You are a happy tree ...
proud to be where you are,
glad to be the way you are.

So, being at one with yourself,
you look across the countryside in front of you ...
you look towards fields of sheep,
fields of cattle,
fields where corn
is turning from green to yellow,
fields where the earth is damp brown
because just today potatoes were harvested,
and you can see sacks stacked together
every 50 yards.

As you look around
you see people coming up the road
on your right hand side ...
about 45 degrees to your right ...
the little narrow road ...
only ever used by tractors,
and children going for a picnic down to the lakeside.

Up this road, towards you,
is coming a group of young men ...

about ten of them.
At first you wonder whether they are the kind
who might break off a branch just for devilment,
or carve their initials on your bark ...
or climb up and sit heavily on you.

But they do not look like that type.
They are smiling ... tired smiles ...
as if they have walked a distance and are weary.

They come closer towards you.
You don't recognize them.
They are not local boys ...
you know that because they are looking at you.
Local folk just walk by.
They are coming closer and looking at you
and one of them –
a man who looks in his late twenties
with jet black hair and a newly trimmed beard –
walks through the group towards you.

You hear him speak ...

JESUS: Yes ... it's a lovely tree.

READER: You appreciate him admiring you.

JESUS: Yes it's a lovely tree.

READER: His eyes are now looking at your branches ...

JESUS: But I'm not looking for beauty.
I'm hungry ... I'm looking for food.

READER: And you think ... well he'll not find any.
It's too early.
I've just got leaves.
I've got the beginnings of flowers on some branches.
Another week and they'll be out.
But no fruit ...

JESUS: I'm hungry, I'm looking for food.

READER: But doesn't he know that it's the wrong season?
Stupid man. Stupid man.

JESUS: Curse you!
Curse you!
From now on ...
From now on, no one ...
No one will ever eat fruit from you again.

(Pause)

READER: And you feel ... in your leaves,
in your branches,
in your roots,
in your self ...
How do you feel?

(Pause)

The man turns his back on you.
His friends look at him in astonishment.
They are silent.
It seems they don't know what to say.
They look at you, almost in sympathy ...
then they walk away, along the road to your left.

One or two of them
occasionally turn their heads and look back ...
but not the man
with the jet black hair and newly trimmed beard.
He doesn't look back ...

He's got other things on his mind ...

He is hungry.

WE DID NOT WANT TO GO

This is the testimony of four followers of Christ who can be found in the Gospels and in the churches today.

It should be read by four people, scattered throughout the worship area, each of whom has a symbol that represents what they are asked to give up.

The symbols should eventually be placed in a visible central location, perhaps on the altar or communion table or on four pedestals. They are put there one by one after each character has spoken and while the congregation sings a response. Alternatively, all can wait until VOICE A says, 'Yet we went'. Then all four can walk to the centre together, place their symbols appropriately and after the words 'We gave up everything and lost more,' say together the last line, 'And we gained the Kingdom of Heaven.'

Prayers may follow, or silence, focused on what we are individually asked to forego for the sake of the Kingdom of Heaven.

SUITABLE SUNG RESPONSE (SEE PAGE 104)
YOUR KINGDOM COME, O LORD (RUSSIAN ORTHODOX)

VOICE A: He called me
but I did not want to go.
I had some business to attend to – private business.

I was a self-made man,
fired by the spirit of free enterprise.

It took a lot of my time, most of my time ...
that's the way it is with private business.

And he expected me to give it up when he called:
give up my independence and go public,
give up competition and go co-operative.

I did not want to go.

(Sung response)

VOICE B: He called me
but I did not want to go.
I had a relationship to attend to –
a private relationship.

I was involved with one person
whom I coveted, adored
and who kept me infatuated ...

that's the way it is with some private relationships.
And he expected me to give it up when he called:
give up my obsession for one person
and love everybody;
give up caring only for one individual
and start caring for the world.

I did not want to go.

(Sung response)

VOICE C: He called me
but I did not want to go.
I had some money to attend to – private money.
I had inherited a small fortune from my parents;

I had made some fast money on the stock market,
and I was making inroads into the black market ...
that's the way it is with private money.

And he expected me to give it up when he called:
give up my private wealth and share it around;
live on less so that others could live on more.

I did not want to go.

(Sung response)

VOICE D: He called me
but I did not want to go.
I had my faith to attend to – my own private faith.

I was devoted to a god
whom I imagined was like me.

I worshipped that god
my own personal way ....

that's the way it is with private faith.
And he expected me to give it up when he called:
give up my private faith and make it public;
serve God in society and not just in my soul.

I did not want to go.

(Sung response)

VOICE A: He called us,
but we did not want to go.

We did not want our business, our love,
our fortune, our faith
to be infected and affected by his touch.

Yet we went.

We gave up everything and lost more.
And we gained the Kingdom of Heaven.

(Sung response)

THE STRANGER

This is a straightforward reading which was originally used in place of a sermon at an evening celebration of Holy Communion in Iona Abbey.

Ideally, it should be used during the six weeks of Eastertide, but there is no restriction to that season.

A Communion hymn may be sung at its conclusion.

READER A: We met him at the close of day ...
the borrowing one we called him ...
and we laughed,
and so did he,
for it was true.

No picnic hamper on his back,
so he borrowed what a boy had,
the bread and fishes boy ...
you'll know the one.

No money in his pocket,
so he borrowed a coin to use in conversation,
the coin with Caesar's head on it ...
you'll know about it.

No place for the Passover,
no food for the meal,
so he borrowed a garret
and cleared the shelves of someone else's pantry:
the upstairs room ...
the bread and wine ...
you'll have heard the story.

And we called him the borrowing one
because he borrowed us ... from our homes,
from our families,
from our jobs ...
and he didn't say he would ever give us back.

It's as if ...
yes, why don't I say it ...
it's as if he presumed that everything,
everyone was his own to call on,
                                       to borrow,
                                       to keep.

(Pause)

READER B: We met him at the close of day ...
the 'stranger' we called him ... and laughed,
for so he was,
and it was true.

Sneaking up behind us
as we walked along the road.
Sneaking? ... no, not sneaking ...
It was as if he had always been there,
that stranger.

Listening to us, ever curious,
ever wanting to make us know that he heard,
that he listened;
and knowing, it seemed, everything,
but letting us say it all first.
Listening? ... no not listening ...
understanding,
that stranger.

And when it came the time
for tired feet to rest under a table,
for bread and wine to be brought, to be shared,
he seemed so at home ...
and so did we.

Strange how he walked with us,
strange how he understood,
strange how the table was the right place
to meet the stranger.

THREE STONE MEDITATIONS

These three meditations may be used singly or, as originally, interspersed with songs and prayers throughout a service.

It is necessary that everyone present has in his or her hand a stone or pebble no larger than a small egg. Stones collected from the beach or a river bed, washed clean, are preferable to granite chips.

During the first two meditations, people should be asked either to look at the stone during the reading or to close their eyes and clutch it in their hand.

In the third mediation, they do not need to focus on the stone, but – if felt appropriate – should hold it in order that at the end of the meditation, they can take their stone and lay it next to a central cross.

A different chant is recommended for each of the meditations.

Please note that the subheadings should not be read out.

SUITABLE SONGS (SEE PAGE 104)
The Stone God Made: O ADORAMUS TE (TAIZÉ)
The Stone the Builders Rejected: BEHOLD THE LAMB OF GOD (WGRG, IONA)
Come as Living Stones: JESU TAWA PANO (ZIMBABWE)

(T H E   S T O N E   G O D   M A D E)

READER A: What I hold in my hand
is as old as me,
and older;

READER B: as old as my name,
my language, my culture,
and older;

READER A: as old as my race,
as old as the human race,
and older;

READER B: as old as the soil,
as old as the sea,
and older;

READER A: as old as the earth,
as old as the sun, moon and stars ...
but younger than God.

READER B: For God made this stone,
made and meant its colour,
its contours,
its journey from below to above.
And had earth never revealed it,
and had I never admired it,
it would still bear witness
to God's deep intention to make the world
mean the world
want the world
wean the world;
and one day, walk the world
and hold in his hand
what I now hold in mine.

(Song: O Adoramus Te)

(THE STONE THE BUILDERS REJECTED)

READER A: This is the stone the builders rejected:

he walked through the wilderness,
through the dry place.
He was thirsty and hungry
and all alone.
As he picked up a stone,
a voice said,
'Turn it to bread.'
And he could have ...
but he let the stone be a stone.

(Behold the Lamb of God)

READER B: This is the stone that the builders rejected:

he came to his own,
but his own would not receive him.

They heard him speak,
heard him open the scriptures,
but would not listen.
'Enough, enough!' they shouted
and took him, stones in hand,
to a hill.

(Behold the Lamb of God)

READER A: This is the stone the builders rejected:

he called those
who had no calling;
He named those
who had no name:
'What you didn't manage with fish
you'll do with people – catch them,' he said.
'They call you simple Simon,
I name you Peter, the rock ...
and on the likes of you ...
on the likes of you,
I'll build my church.'

(Behold the Lamb of God)

READER B: This is the stone that the builders rejected:

he bent down
to touch the ground,
to cradle children,
to kneel with one whom all despised.
'Throw your stones,' he said,
'Throw them at her;
and let the flawless fling theirs first.'
They went away, stones in hand,
for another day and for him.

(Behold the Lamb of God)

READER A: This is the stone the builders rejected:

he was edged out of the world,
        onto the cross,
        into a tomb.
And a stone was stationed
to keep the dead away from the living,
but the stone was rolled away
for death was rejected.
Death died
and the stone was rolled away.

(Behold the Lamb of God)

(C O M E   A S   L I V I N G   S T O N E S)

READER A: 'Come,' says God, 'as living stones.
        You are the chosen race.'

READER B: But, Lord, you know our trouble –
        the pace.

We are fools
who work full time.

We are do-ers
who are overdone.
We are a tired race,
        a fallen race,
        a busy race.

READER A: 'Come ... you are the chosen race.'

(Jesu Tawa Pano)

READER A: 'Come,' says God, 'as living stones.
        You are the King's priests.'

READER C: But, Lord, you know our trouble –
        we are not royal or religious.

We are commoners
who enjoy insignificance.
We are lay people
who criticize the clergy.

We are the faithless,
    the faltering,
    the least.

READER A: 'Come ... you are my priests.'

(Jesu Tawa Pano)

READER A: 'Come,' says God, 'as living stones.
You are the holy nation.'

READER D: But, Lord, you know our trouble –
we are not guiltless.

We are the people
who pray for peace, yet arm for war.
We are the people
who bemoan pollution, yet poison the earth.
We are the people
who disparage poverty, yet bleed the poor.

We are a selfish nation,
    an indulgent nation,
    a proud nation.

READER A: 'Come ... you are a holy nation.'

(Jesu Tawa Pano)

You ... and you ... and you ...
are God's own people,
chosen to proclaim the acts of God
who called you out of darkness
into his marvellous light.
Once you were no people.
Now you are God's people.

(Jesu Tawa Pano – during this people may if they wish bring their stones and lay them in commitment round a centrally positioned cross.)

GOD'S OWN PEOPLE

1 Peter 2 is a magnificent affirmation of how God chooses those who seem least worthy and least special to be the people to whom he gives much and from whom he expects great things.

Here is a quite straightforward reading of verses from the scripture which, if enhanced by simple actions, can be a very compelling experience.

The congregation should stand for the reading with the reader almost in their midst, able to address them eye-to-eye with the words of this letter. The reader should speak with the kind of warmth and encouragement which underlies the words, pausing where indicated so that the congregation may respond in song.

Four people should stand behind the leader near a table or tables on which there are four lighted candles per assistant. These should not be small votive lights, but preferably 24-hour lights in plastic holders.

When it comes to the point where the reader says 'You are the chosen race' each assistant takes one candle and goes into the congregation, seeks out someone who might least expect it and, handing her or him the candle, repeats the words, 'You are the chosen race.'

The assistants all return to their places before the reader proceeds with the next lines which are followed with similar activity.

SUITABLE SONG (SEE PAGE 104)
SANTO / HOLY, HOLY, HOLY (ARGENTINA)

READER: Let there be no more lying or hypocrisy
or jealous talk or insulting language.
You've to become like new born babies,
thirsty for the pure spiritual milk,
so that by drinking it, you may be saved.

Remember what the scripture says:
'You have found out for yourselves
how kind the Lord is.'

(Sung response)

READER: Come to the Lord,
the living stone,
rejected by men and women as worthless,
but chosen by God as valuable.
Come and let yourselves be used
in building his spiritual temple.

Remember what the scripture says:
'I'm placing a corner stone in Zion.
Whoever believes in him
will never be disappointed.'

(Sung response)

READER: This is what God says,
'You are the chosen race.'

ASSISTANTS: *(Moving to individuals and giving them candles)*
You are the chosen race.

READER: 'You are the King's priests.'

ASSISTANTS: *(As above)* You are the King's priests

READER: 'You are the holy nation.'

ASSISTANTS: *(As above)* You are the holy nation.

READER: 'You are God's own people.'

ASSISTANTS: *(As above)* You are God's own people.

READER: 'You are chosen ...
chosen to proclaim the wonderful work of God
who has called you out of darkness
into his marvellous light.

Once you were no people;
now you are God's people.

Once you never knew his mercy;
now you have received it.'

*A*ppendix

ILLUSTRATIONS FOR PHOTOCOPYING

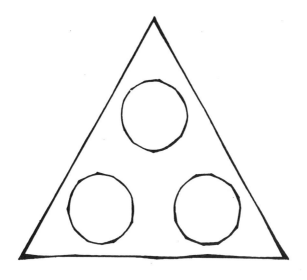

THE SAINTS OF GOD

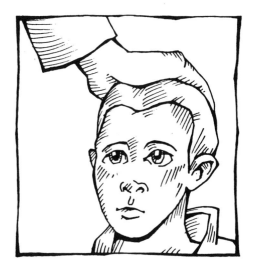

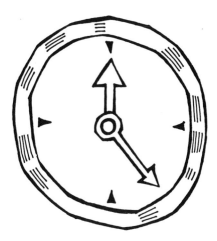

LAZARUS (5)

S ources of recommended songs

BE STILL AND KNOW (WGRG, Iona Community)
Enemy of Apathy (Wild Goose Publications, Glasgow 1988)

BEHOLD THE LAMB OF GOD (WGRG, Iona Community)
Enemy of Apathy (Wild Goose Publications, Glasgow 1988)

BLESS THE LORD MY SOUL (Taizé)
Songs and Prayers from Taizé (Geoffrey Chapman/Mowbray 1991)
Songs of God's People (Oxford University Press 1988)

COME HOLY SPIRIT (WGRG, Iona Community)
Enemy of Apathy (Wild Goose Publications, Glasgow 1988)

HE BECAME POOR (WGRG, Iona Community)
Love from Below (Wild Goose Publications, Glasgow 1989)

JESU TAWA PANO (Zimbabwe)
Many and Great (Wild Goose Publications, Glasgow 1990)

KYRIE ELEISON (Ghana)
Many and Great (Wild Goose Publications, Glasgow 1990)

O ADORAMUS TE (Taizé)
Songs and Prayers from Taizé (Geoffrey Chapman/Mowbray 1991)

O LORD, HEAR MY PRAYER (Taizé)
Songs and Prayers from Taizé (Geoffrey Chapman/Mowbray 1991)
Songs of God's People (Oxford University Press 1988)

SANTO / HOLY, HOLY, HOLY (Argentina)
Many and Great (Wild Goose Publications, Glasgow 1990)

UBI CARITAS ET AMOR (Taizé)
Songs and Prayers from Taizé (Geoffrey Chapman/Mowbray 1991)
Songs of God's People (Oxford University Press 1988)

WATCH AND PRAY (WGRG, Iona Community)
Enemy of Apathy (Wild Goose Publications, Glasgow 1988)

YOUR KINGDOM COME, O LORD (Russian Orthodox)
Many and Great (Wild Goose Publications, Glasgow 1990)